Quiet

Quiet

Poems

VICTORIA ADUKWEI BULLEY

ALFRED A. KNOPF
New York
2023

THIS IS A BORZOI BOOK PUBLISHED BY ALFRED A. KNOPF

Copyright © 2022 by Victoria Adukwei Bulley

All rights reserved. Published in the United States by Alfred A. Knopf,
a division of Penguin Random House LLC, New York, and distributed in Canada
by Penguin Random House Canada Limited, Toronto. Originally published in
Great Britain by Faber & Faber Limited, London, in 2022.

www.aaknopf.com

Knopf, Borzoi Books, and the colophon are
registered trademarks of Penguin Random House LLC.

Selected poems first appeared in the following publications: "Death is Everywhere
& Not Here" (*Ambit,* 2017); "[   ] noise" (*bath magg,* 2021); "six weeks," "Dreaming
is a Form of Knowledge Production," and "The Ultra-Black Fish" (*Granta,* 2022); "Air" (*The
Guardian,* 2022); "Whose Name Means Honey" (*Magma,* April 2022); "Stephanie" (*MAP
Magazine,* 2020); "What it Means" (*The Rialto,* 2016); "ode" (*London Review of Books,* 2020);
"About Ana" and "revision" (*Tongue,* 2017); "Retreat" and "Girls in Arpeggio"
(*Ten: Poets of the New Generation,* 2017); "essex playground, 2004" (*Stand,* 2022);
"dear little b," (*The Nation,* 2022); "Epigenetic," "Declaration," and "not quiet as
in quiet but" (*ZYZZYVA,* 2022); and "Leavetaking" originally
aired on the *Poets in Bed* podcast in 2019.
The image on page 74 that forms part of "fabula"
was created by the author and Timothy Pulford-Cutting.

Library of Congress Cataloging-in-Publication Data
Names: Bulley, Victoria Adukwei, author.
Title: Quiet : poems / Victoria Adukwei Bulley.
Description: First American edition. | New York : Alfred A. Knopf, 2023.
Summary: "A thrilling Black British poet making her American debut explores the importance
of "quiet" in producing forms of community, resistance, and love"—Provided by publisher.
Identifiers: LCCN 2022029540 (print) | LCCN 2022029541 (ebook) |
ISBN 9780593535646 (hardcover) | ISBN 9780593535653 (ebook)
Subjects: LCGFT: Poetry.
Classification: LCC PR6102.U436 Q54 2023 (print) | LCC PR6102.U436 (ebook) |
DDC 821/.92—dc23/eng/20220705
LC record available at https://lccn.loc.gov/2022029540
LC ebook record available at https://lccn.loc.gov/2022029541

Jacket painting by Abe Odedina / Ed Cross Fine Art, UK
Jacket design by Linda Huang

Manufactured in the United States of America
First American Edition

For my mother, who dreamed me first

It is this exploration, this reach toward the inner life, that an aesthetic of quiet makes possible; and it is this that is the path to a sweet freedom: a black expressiveness without publicness as its forbearer, a black subject in the undisputed dignity of its humanity.

—KEVIN QUASHIE

". . . you got to hold tight a place in you where they can't come."

—ALICE WALKER

Contents

A DOOR, A KEY

Declaration

if sickness begins in the gut, if

       I live in the belly of the beast, if

here at the heart of empire—

       if careful in the house of the host, if

       quiet at the hearth of the host, if

here at the home of empire—

       if I live in the belly of the beast,

let me beget sickness in its gut.

Declaration: I

check if you want to

but you won't find any

lyric shame here.

we don't do that, no;

we nuh ave dat here.

you won't find one lash

on the surface of this eye—

look: if I say I, I mean

a lot of people

& at this table

all of us eat.

ROOM OF CONDITIONS & REFUSALS

As black people we exist metaphorically and literally as the underside, the underclass. We are the unconscious of the entire Western world. If this is in fact true, then where do we go? Where are our dreams? Where is our pain? Where do we heal?

—NTOZAKE SHANGE

revision

i. consider

from the 1400s, the area later known as *the gold coast* would be (choose one)
discovered / invaded / visited / landed upon
by
europeans / illegal aliens / migrant workers / tourists / christians
hailing from the ports of
sweden / denmark / england / the netherlands / portugal / prussia

during their
visit / residency / occupation / sabbatical / stay
they would alter, irreversibly, the
ecology / lives / speech / gods / memory
of the
homo sapiens / natives / people / fauna
inhabiting the land. it is not clear   what their expectations were.
                    one could assume   they were successful.
even after
completing / losing / leaving / tiring of   the project & going home
                    it is arguable that   they did not actually   leave.

ii. compare

A   <u>onion</u>   *'sabolai'*   hint: cebola

B   *'chalé'*   charlie   hint: fam

C   hint: water bird   <u>duck</u>   *'dokor-dokor'*

D   *'lala'*   hint: ♫   <u>song</u>

iii. consolidate

in the year of our lord
1471
they came—

in the year of our lord
2017
i look for my language,

still finding in it
their hairs.

iv. conclude

oh *chalé!*
i stayed in portugal for a year & loved it. loved it. more than england, fam. patriot,
who? water off a duck's back. two colonisers: one with better weather—what's the
problem. the people were happy. it was hot. i stayed in bolhão. i'd go to the market
& buy vegetables & come back to the apartment & make rice & stew. i do that
when i want to feel at home. i like to think that i can bring home with me. & you
know i can't speak ga, but our word for onion is *sabolai*. right? & the portuguese
word for onion? *cebola*. say-ball-ah. i love it. i love it & i hate it, & this year it
happened again. this very january. mum played me a video of grandma singing a
folk tune, & she told me that the word for 'song' in ga is *lala*. lala. as in, *deck the
halls with boughs of holly, fa-la-la-la-la* can you believe that? & i was so happy to
see grandma so alive, singing all these words—of which i understand nothing—
see her clapping, all nearly-one-hundred-&-fully-bat-blind years of her, & even
mum didn't know the story, she just translated the outline to me, which i don't
remember now, but the whole time i could only stand there, i was just watching &
thinking damn, this *lala* feels sad, this one *lala* sounds like a sorry song

Lost Belonging

I
left
my bag
on the train
under the table.
Forgot it, looking
at the sun as I rolled
home into the city. Gold
was spilling from the frame
of a skyscraper & it looked
like a fire but it was only nature
reflecting off of steel. It was nature,
at it again, refracting from the metals
of this skin that we have grown so lately.
Everything is going to break & I must get
home before it does, or doesn't yet, or buckles.
Back to the locked shut door, to the batteries +/−
all dashed from the clock, & the blinds closed tight,
a millipede of stinging eyes, red light crashing through
from the place behind them.   *Mother,*   *where else can I go?*

girl

hair coming down past your breasts like confetti. your straighter teeth, your stripped upper lip (recoiling still), your clean, dark complexion. lean legs, or the gap between them. the grasp of your jeans at you like a lover that you'd like to leave, exposing the gap. the sign between your feet pointing upwards, *tear here*. sun, sea, sand, shea butter, you are smoother skin, polished nails, dark eyes: seeing-almonds. your voice, your vocal cords, stroked by secondhand smoke. your dozy tongue, stacking it over words you really should know how to pronounce by now. & feet, lithe, slim, no peeling, arches secure as scaffolds. oiled joints, humming the silence of youth. limbs fighting baby jihads against lipids; still winning. your heart still kicking it in time, red metronome, your shunning of the night; a propensity for wakefulness, for pen against paper—a dance of sorts—because what is death to you?

(break)

my sweet girl.

(break)

will you write to me, years from today, when you no longer are what you are now? i'd like to know what you'll be.

(break)

call me when you find out.

(break)

i'll be here.

essex playground, 2004

the boys round here
    the ones that look like you
    don't love the look of you
they like the orange girls
    the ones who wear foundation
    like rapture is any minute & satan
    might crawl out of the ground in essex, wearing
    JOOP! & bearing handbags
the ones who turn & flick their hair so it cracks
    like whips on the minds of these boys
    the boys that you like
    the ones that look like you
       & your brothers.

Girls in Arpeggio

1. *Early Intervention*

The smiles of the girls
on the children's relaxer kits
told no lies. They were too happy
to realise they were poster girls
for the effacement of themselves.

Being none the wiser
we would sit there, still,
watching our mothers mix dreams
with a spatula; watching the mirror
from under the eaves
of our alkaline cream hats. We stared
at the girl on the box, willing
to be cleaned, even before sin,

& as the soft, pink science got working,
pleasantly tickling the skin, we waited
until our blood-borne bonds would break
just enough, perhaps,
for all in the world that resisted us
to straighten out.

2. Forbearance

There is a toll charged
for choosing to be the exotic one.

The problem has something to do
with your acceptance of a cage
made from laundered gold.

> *birds of paradise,*
> *you were the first dreams to die*
> *when the ships arrived . . .*

3. *Forgiveness*

Oh Daughters of Eve,
did you know that you
were quarter-formed things?

Or did you never pull the wings
from a fly, one by one, & wonder
what to call it then?

Or did they only tell you & tell you
walk tall, hold your heads high
you sweeter berries,

you picked-too-soons
& placed in the heat to dry
& stain the pavement

apologetically.

4. *Realpolitik*

Somewhere beyond the last of the pencil lines   tattooed
onto the doorframes of their kitchens,   their only nations,   these girls,
cacao-cored & peppercorn pin-curled, decided to call themselves   *beautiful.*
Not chocolate or caramel.   Not coconut or tan.   Not Bounty,
not Hovis best-of-both or burnt wholegrain toast. Not buff nor carbon-cum-diamond
blick. Not lighty, not hair enough to hang from.   Not video girl.   Not
side-chick. Not thick,   not booty or apple-bottom.   Not deputation any
longer, not another   word   not vice not hereafter
          any cover-teacher   or stand-in nor prefix; no sign nor understudy
no other   for *beauty*   anymore.

For these girls it was a violent act.
Afterwards, they slept better.

Fifteen

With his hopscotch grid for a wrist
see my blue boy

with a smile like a one-string guitar,
relative to nobody,

dropping out of school,
out of line, saying

I love you more than life itself
in a first Valentine's card

during the term
in which we turn fifteen.

In the attic of an old phone, now,
here he is again

in the drawer I was emptying
during a hymn I was singing

before I met him
& here he is, my blue boy—

now watch this older girl stop
& throw her day out with the dust

& turn blue, too.

This whole impermanence thing is deceptive.
Looks lifelong, actually, to me

still stuck here moulding Mason jars
of words to preserve him with,

wondering if a poem ten years on
is still a pining, asking

how many more I'll make
having learned, at last,

how little of us keeps.

not quiet as in quiet but

as in peaceful /
as in slow to anger /
as in shy /
as in sulking or sullen /
as in nice /
as in clean, tree-lined streets /
as in well-resourced libraries /
as in good, outstanding schools /
as in not much new /
as in no news is good news /
as in the war is over; has been for decades now /
as in early to bed / curled up with a book /
as in the newborn is sleeping /
as in TV barely audible /
as in subtitles /
as in subtext /
as in someone should've done something /
as in don't just do something, stand there /
as in could & should but wouldn't /
as in well the British are / so polite /
as in placid /
as in placated /
as in nuanced / complicated /
as in careful it's a conflict, not a siege, a conflict /
as in objective /
as in both sides /
as in well behaved /
as in safe /
as in too quiet /
as in almost silent /
as in almost no sirens /

How Not to Disappear

'I told a police officer that my son was missing, please help me find him, and she said: "If you can't find your son, how do you expect police officers to find your son for you?"'

Who would guess the prayers you'll say
walking home at night, crossing streets you know
too well were never yours to claim. All the promises
you'll make about what you'll do with your life
should you make it to the warm indoors,
the soft & grateful bed. *God*, you'll say, below your breath,
let no strange man put hands on me, let the dark
not drape this body on terms other than its own;
speed me to the door, let the first key be the right one;
the mechanism oiled & easy. *& should I fail*, you'll say
*in any of this, let me have spoken to no one lately
about bad days, hard times*, or worse have written
a poem or two about them, to be found when your belongings
are thumbed through, finally; too late. *Please, God*, you'll say,
one more time, deliver me home to my known life, seen
& loved by those to whom it's always mattered; borne & fed
by a lover & others who, like you, already know how
(& how not) to disappear, unable to forget
the way they spoke to that boy's mother.

What it Means

The campus nurse, she means it
when she says it's one less thing to worry about.

& that's okay:
there are many freedoms.

In her world
freedom from bloodshed

is tasted
between the legs.

I don't judge.
How would she know

I have come to love
the cup spilling over:

the floor of the bath
a Rothko on fibreglass

an opening ceremony
a private showing

circa this month.
There is little like knowing

I am an orchestra—
only rehearsing.

About Ana

The truth is, nobody
        knows how Ana Mendieta
met her death. It would appear
        she was pushed. Some distance below,
the doorman said he heard
        a woman shout No, & then
the sound as her body
        hit the top of the deli
so hard her face left a mark
        like a metal stamp. In the photo
she is naked & feathered. She looks
        like the first woman,
like she doesn't know
        what a camera is, that somewhere
in the world it is believed
        these things can steal a soul.
Her arms are out, as if to say
        you move them like this, to fly—
like this, *sí?* Her feet are
        apart, you can see the sphere
of her hips, the delta between
        her legs. I look at her, sated, & think *this*
is the true work of the body,
        to adorn itself & be comfortable,
unaware. I myself am bored
        of fig leaves, of shames
I did not choose.

This Poem

Somewhere beneath this poem
    is the one you sat down to write.
        Locked into the hold of it, or running
    shaded, through the leaves of this book
is the poem that escaped untouched
    by hands that know no tenderness.
        This poem is not that poem.
    Not the one you travelled for.
This poem is *this* poem, you concede,
    the one that took your hand instead.
        & being here now, having journeyed already so far
    you sit down with this poem to talk.
& you are silent as you listen
    to the stories it speaks of, which are not yours
        though you are in them, though they contain you
    all the same. & when you write that other
poem, the one you promised to meet, still
    you hear this one's cruel whisperings
        as it floats in the air,
    as it lights on the shelf
        & waits there, watching,
          rubbing its hands
            like a fly.

[   ] noise

& even when we said we were alone there was [   ] noise on the radio & there was [   ] noise in the car & there was [   ] noise all over the internet & there was [   ] noise in the atmosphere & there was [   ] noise trapped in the system & there was [   ] noise in the economy & [   ] noise was the economy & there was [   ] noise on the train & there was [   ] noise on the road & there was [   ] noise at the board meeting & there was [   ] noise on the field & there was [   ] noise on the kitchen counter & [   ] noise in the cutlery drawer & there was [   ] noise at the hospital where there was [   ] noise in the blood & there was [   ] noise in the water supply & there was [   ] noise in the ocean & there was [   ] noise eating the ice caps & the polar bears were drowning because of it & washed up on the beaches then was a morbid & off-white [   ] noise & there was [   ] noise in the street & there was [   ] noise in the ozone a whole hole's worth of [   ] noise just counting down the days & there was [   ] noise in the photos of us because [   ] noise was on the lens & there was [   ] noise on the brain scan & there was [   ] noise during the exam where there was [   ] noise scratched into the desk & there was [   ] noise in the texts & there was [   ] noise in the census & there was [   ] noise in the law & there was [   ] noise on Friday at the cinema & there was [   ] noise at the seminar & there was [   ] noise at the peace talks & there was [   ] noise in the rent & there was [   ] noise on the wellness podcast & there was [   ] noise in the obituary & there were little [   ] noise cookies remaining even after carefully choosing *reject all* & there was [   ] noise in the inquest & there was [   ] noise in the commission & there was [   ] noise in the system you hear because [   ] noise was the system & too [   ] noise was reform & there was [   ] noise in the wounding & there was [   ] noise in the wording of the apology the [   ] noisiness of which made entirely void the apology & there was [   ] noise in the diversity statement & there was [   ] noise in the group chat & there was [   ] noise in the joke of it all, there was [   ] noise in the delivery & there was [   ] noise in the returns process & in the practice & in the prayer & it was there in the room with us still even when we said we were alone even when we swore that we could not hear it

Death is Everywhere & Not Here

when the happiest girl I know plays songs by a group called the Deep
Throat Choir. & while the others at the bar can't stand it, but won't tell
her to her face, I imagine telling strangers my new occupation—brazen
& unfazed by the name of my band. These days, *everything* moves. The white
hair I rip from my scalp at the middle parting turns out to be black at its root
meaning: it changed its follicle mind for a whole centimetre, or six weeks
(depending on who's counting). I, too, want space & time & second chances.
I want to be useful & beautiful but what did I do today except watch a tall
building burn, while the boy who once called it home phones the BBC, says
you know at least five hundred people live in there—I didn't see five hundred people leave
with a voice that implies this is a normal day for him. Death, I think it's you
I face when a spider crosses my path in a place I thought was mine. Is it not
you who turns overhead with no warning, declaring the night an open disco?
There will always be more of you to kill or free. There will not always be mothers
with brooms, fathers with cups or glasses, there will not always even be empty
glasses—there will not always even be anyone, only there will be you, death, &
the silence & the shade as the audience traps breath to ask *is this it, will the music
play now, will the credits roll*, before leaving the cinema, eyes learning daylight again,
rebirthing the world, heads brim-full in the interim of everything to do
& nothing to be done

A SEAL, A KEY

Epigenetic

Maybe it's nuts but it helps sometimes
      to think that here
in the ridges of these fingernails
      someone in this blood thinks it's shit
what we've settled for; is shocked
      to a stupor by what they see: the trouble
we've seen; the more of it coming.
      Someone with this mouth, these dark lips
is watching the screen of my vision
      & screaming at it. I believe in this
& what it poses, makes possible—

    Dear astigmatism—

Dear tastebuds—

    Dear—

    someone not far away, but here.
Not gone or geologic, but now
      & *really here*—denser-boned
& better-sunned than I; raised on maize
      not wheat. Some she, some they, some he
or other, in these hundred thousand hairs
      these ten pints of blood
is pained by the cruel audacity of this;
      hysterical in no good way.
I do believe,
    I do believe—

      Dear earlobes—

Dear little toes—

        Dear lines on my palms—

Dear sideburns—

        Dear serotonin—we don't have long—

Dear plasma—

        Dear earwax, it must be true—

    someone written in you
still knows what it felt like—
    our life otherwise than this—
if your pain is alive in me
    so too must be your joy.

There You Are

There you are
this cold day
boiling the water on the stove
pouring the herbs into the pot
hawthorn, rose;
buying the tulips
& looking at them, holding
your heart in your hands at the table
saying *please, please,* to nobody else
here in the kitchen with you.
How hard, how heavy this all is.
How beautiful, these things you do,
in case they help, these things you do
which, although you haven't said it yet,
say that you want to live.

INTERIORS

There is a basin in the mind where words float around on thought and thought on sound and sight. Then there is a depth of thought untouched by words, and deeper still a gulf of formless feelings untouched by thought.
—ZORA NEALE HURSTON

"Girl, I got my mind. And what goes on in it. Which is to say, I got me."
—TONI MORRISON

black noise

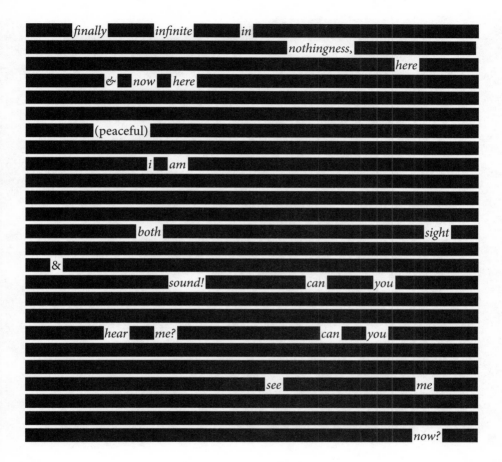

finally   infinite   in
nothingness,
here
&   now   here

(peaceful)

i   am

both   sight
&
sound!   can   you

hear   me?   can   you

see   me

now?

Whose Name Means Honey

You are beautiful to me.
You are beautiful to me
across the table we have arrived at,
in from the rain; no make-up on your face
but for the small frail thread
of something on your right cheek
that I would like to remove for you,
you whose name
means *honey*. Every time
you look up
& still it is there, I would like
to be the one who says *hold on,*
come here, let me, one minute, stay there,
almost, there we go, all done, perfect. & when
you look up & now it is gone, swept
absent-mindedly off the face of the earth
by your dark hair, oh I am sad
to have missed my chance

Retreat

4
Ruby says nothing.
Ruby cuts a tube of penne in half with the side of her fork, a slow-motion blade
stooping to kiss the back of my neck. A warning. *Eat, before it gets cold; before you
forget how to do it.* Until now, I jigsawed her exposition to find the best fit.
Satisfied, I clean my plate.

3
I haven't seen a wasp in years, but there are *wasps* here, larger than the ones
I remember. Padma, our retreat leader, climbs the bunk bed, removes a hornet
from the room with a cup.

2
Evan is a sixty-five-year-old retired father, just like Dad. *You remind me of my dad,*
I tell him, *the only difference being, of course, that you're white.*

4
Everybody has bought & is studying one of the many dharma books on sale here,
except Alastair, 84, who reads Alistair Cooke, instead.

5
I am in the shrine room, closest to Buddha, when Evan is crying. We two are the last
ones left, but the room—though vacant—is loud with her, humming *Susan, Susan,*
between each caught breath.

1
The week begins when I turn off my phone. I delete the world as an infant does.
I keep my palms flush over my eyes, until I realise I do not own a watch
or an alarm clock.

6

Brother, may you be well. May you be happy. May you be free from suffering.

7

On the last evening, a sunset. My turn in the kitchen. Ruby offers to take my shift, so that I can walk with the others. It is the first time she's volunteered to speak to me, & when she calls me, I hear it like a song, & begin to love my name.

8

Barbara waves until the rear-view mirror swings her face & wind-up hand out of sight. I will see her again, several times. I don't know this. Or, too, that she will even visit my house, sit with me on the floor of my parents' room, where it is quiet. Or that whenever I picture her, no matter how much in the future, she will always be waving goodbye.

six weeks

what if I gave you a name, & it made remembering easier. I am a person who tries to keep things. I am a girl, also, who forgets she is a woman nowadays, with a body that does womanly things, at times undoes them, unfastens the sound *wuu-man* like a cord from around the neck.

had a heartbeat, lost it. had a mind, almost, then changed it. at six weeks, a heart begins to beat, like a coin starting to roll, a new idea, a lightbulb, a streetlamp turning on at dusk just as you pass it walking home.

how often does this happen?

all of this made us want you; made you wantable & imminent.

& then,
something other in me, or you, or the universe, had a change of heart, tugged the rope
a little harder & won. & there, finally, like that: the meaning of dialectics. the inner
workings of things not visible to us. only their push & pull being felt, & us the children
in the divorce. forces we know are there but can't see; five senses not nearly enough.
known unknowns that make us humble ourselves, choose the right place in the
hierarchy & hold out our hands for what is not promised—

. . . in the empty space, I want to think of you deliberately. do something.
create a national holiday in your namelessness, in my head.
close the banks & write a poem. burn a candle. buy a plant & water it.

when you fell, warm, into my hand I put you into a jar. wrapped the jar in newspaper. placed it on the dressing table & slept, awed, across the room, non-dreaming. when I woke up, I put you into the fridge.

the nurse's name was Valentine, Zimbabwean, & so kind I called her *auntie*. the train I write this from is passing a cemetery now. I am more used to travelling in darkness but today I see it: the place for everything in life. literal, not figurative, the graves—with my eyes I take them in. I would like to walk between them, slowly, leaving brief & careful tellings on the air with my breath.

date with no entry

every way to deep it, but no way to swim.

natally wounded comes to mind.

it had a nice ring to it; it left the mouth well.

when you've done enough, are you the last to know?

sometimes the whole operating system is faulty.

what are the subscriptions left to cancel?

junk mail aplenty; no *click here to unsubscribe.*

no idea who gave the devil your details.

it's not you this time, it's the planets that are mad.

you're okay, really, you just caught a ghost.

what's yours is yours. what's theirs is yours too. (a sadness so heavy.)

a sadness so heavy.

sticky & gumlike, colour-fast.

ignore & it will stay forever, loyal to you.

act too soon & you'll seal it in for good.

scrubbing your bedsheets in the bathroom in shame.

sweetheart, sweetheart,

when you've had enough, will you be the last to know?

is it love that you're seeking, or permission?

what will you choose when you can't have both?

is it true, is it useful: *a sadness so heavy.*

a sorrow like this needs washing on its own terms.

the answer: not always hot water.

turn on both taps, & cup your hands under.

like in prayer, but open.

not right or wrong, but left & right: both you.

wash your loss at the body's own temperature.

observe how, like blood, now it runs.

toby

your ears move
even when you are asleep:
you sleep with two eyes open.

*

he: small matador. he: sometimes cerebral. aspirational puma. part-time mirther. never moist, not ever. osmosis-like, he moves through air; his slumber, an amber stupor with a keepsake tint. little simba, quiet alba. tabby *à la* al-ʿAttābīyya, he: my small-town glitch in the isotope of the morning.

*

though he leaps at what may appear to us as nothing, be not fooled, for verily he
 catches it.

*

like so:
busy, practising true self.
busy, *ad infinitum*, knowing crystalline what that is.

*

babycat, my love! I've swept the whole flat
& look how much of you I've combed
from under the sofa, beneath the dining table,
from the fibres of the sitting room rug. I sweep,
I sweep again & you are uncontainable, unmatched, I say,
there is such power in your immanence, I think it is
or just might be a miracle, babycat,
how you let yourself fall like this
& never once die.

*

THOUGHT: [bright & exuberant] *Maybe he's born with it!*
SECOND THOUGHT: [waits a beat, then nods]

*

see him splayed in the shade of the patio.
he must not suffer, so we offer water & ice.
if he would let us, we would shave him like a poodle
& mop the sweat from the M of his brow.

*

well, me? I'm not no one.

but he has knives
& they are worth something.

when he says *No*, he means it.
look how he says so like a blade means blood.

*

hey baby, I like the way you wake me in the morning before dawn, pawing the French windows to be let back in, even though I sleep, even though I'm all at sea in dreams, you know? babycat of course it's not rude of you, it's not rude of you at all, to know what you want & go get it—& what a go-getter you are, oh yes doesn't the world just love folks like you! I wasn't dreaming of much anyway, & can't remember now anyhow, sweet furry thing, it's no bother. really. you wanted out so I let you out. then you wanted in & so I let you in. whatever you want, you insist upon it & that's what we call: assertiveness! sheer CONFIDENCE, babycat. won't you catch a little for me & lay it at my feet still breathing? oh babycat, won't you one fine day please bring me some of that?

Pandemic vs Black Folk

It never was a virus that came for us, not really.
Don't ask me what my mother knows about that.
If yours never told you, perhaps we can't be friends.
We always were too welcoming a people, or so it's said,
or should I say, *peoples*. Plural as the distance between leaf
& leaves; as the difference between twig & tree—what we were
before being rolled into singular, brought to the flame & lit
for an inhale that hasn't ended. Who are *your* peoples?
If we need to know, we'll ask who sent you. If you're suspect,
we'll ask where you're *really* from. If you're safe, we'll bring water
on a tray, say: *sit down, wash your hands, eat.* It never was a virus
that killed us, no, not even if it killed en masse. Worse things
have happened at sea, or so it goes. & if anybody knows that, we do.

Suddenly, all across the land, this great land,
this dunya, this Great Britain, this Britain First,
this Brexit means Brexit so fresh & so green
green & pleasant land, it seems there is no toilet roll,
no soap. As if the Moors came & snatched it back,
astaghfirullah. Shelves good as new—empty as the day
they were built. Meanwhile, in the canned food aisle, nary
a tin of tomatoes to be found. I guess it's good folks
are learning how to cook. A prayer for our elders, who
only stepped out for fresh air. There's rice at home yet
for the time being. As for toilet paper, that's a different thing.
If cleanliness were godliness all along, no Columbus could have
made the New World new. If cleanliness were godliness, really,
there would be soap in the shops even now.

Things being still early, we hug first & remember second.
Arms are thrown about backs, fingers gesture towards
hair, admiring a careful day's work of braids.
Cue laughter as usual, cue knowing smiles—
& what is it that we feel, beneath all this, that gives
our meetings their sugared ease? Not denial, quite.
Not humour to evade dissemblance this time.
The body keeps a logbook of what happens to it.
Bones can speak long after the flesh has gone. Often,
on the train, the one seat that's free is the one
that's next to me & that's just fine. You know a girl
likes a space to place her bag. Maybe social distancing
is another way of saying that. Yes. *When I walk into a room
I never know what I might do*. In this skin, sis, I'm a virus too.

ode

oh my diablo, diablo pequeño, oh night singer, oh most true & high falsetto, oh
starving four-winged mother, oh lone she-wolf, oh once nymph, oh primordial
stagnation, oh explorador, oh lover of house reds, oh witching hour jinn, oh erratic,
oh evasive, oh god no & now unmistakeable, oh warm & international, oh unlikely but
not impossible death deliveroo, oh most consistent, oh highly dependent, oh addict,
oh seeker of beautiful veins, oh collector of DNA, oh genome stealer, oh cartographer
of blood, oh rogue scientist, oh government pawn, oh infiltrator, oh infidel, oh drone,
oh promised one, oh midnight kiss, oh lovebite perfectly circular & raised a little,
oh long-nailed orgasmic itch, oh ooze, oh souvenir, oh scar, oh skin constellation,
oh BioOil boomer, oh money maker, oh leg slapper, oh clap & check both hands,
oh newspaper, oh towel, oh book or whatever's closer, oh dream breaker, oh organic
alarm, oh call to arms, oh supplicant, oh rogue, oh swift invasion, oh awful tenant, oh
short-term lease, oh tiny [   ] man with bugle to scale, oh poacher, oh crosshair,
oh ear worm, oh fish hook tonight I am bait & I tried but will not win! oh coloniser,
tonight I am the island you'll name with your mouth as you must, as you must, make
it quick & noiseless just take my shit & go

Leavetaking

Summer in October & for sure now, the world is ending.
A fruit that caught its mould from another, too soon.
All the same, the grass glows with our belongings, a jade beach
Satin-bright in the sun with our shed nightwear.
& my palm shading your eyes from the glare: a kindness.
Your hand at the fork of my body, this too, affectionate.
We have returned to the earth early. How it loves us for this.
How it considers us family, pulls us in as its own.
So in awe that when we stand the ground will keep our shape.
Such reverence that when we rise, the grass stays down impressed
& passers-by will wonder what happened here; if we lived.
So kind these things we do with & for & to one another.
So standing to attention & generous, complicit—
Selfish, & unspeakable but pyjama-hysteric; imperative
In the morning, at midday, in the tenth month of the year.
I want to say the weather breaks my heart but it doesn't.
The plane overhead will circle back around like any old grief.
We offer our bodies to it like art for the best view.
Here we are, gone, finished, so scrutable beyond saving.
Here are we, way out beyond the wash & nobody coming.
Here is where we admit what we won't say with our mouths
Say, instead, tongue to opening, thigh to ear, fold to fold, how we know
We aren't going to fix the world & no one is coming. & here,
How we cope: one hundred million of you flung out onto the lawn.
A pointillistic offering—no two the same. In our leave-taking, we do
What we can. The hedges are high enough. Your neighbours, long dead.
We step out of our bodies & into the light.

Stephanie

I walked past your house today
on the way to mine

I thought I might stop by again
& we could talk a little or too long

until late preferably
until my phone rings—

somebody was in your porch
calling to someone else inside

who was maybe your mother, your sister
or even yourself

& I thought about stopping by
but it wasn't your mother's car

in the drive & no it wasn't
your house anymore.

We would walk to the park at night-time.
I would tell you to quit your job.

What is a friend
but someone to sit with

on the swings
out in the darkness.

A SEAL, A DOOR

Declaration

    & should you watch me stop my mouth

it is only   to save my breath   for singing

     in the world to come

              & should you see me hold

                      my tongue

it is to better speak a language

    among those with whom

        it might be shared

Dedication

to fill the fissure

        with gold

to bear   no enemies

      to lose

          no time

refuse   to whip   the self.

        to wash

   the I

     the vision   clear

the sea

  still

     the tide   high

  to watch

      the eye

to be   —become

        responsible.

   we are always

      accountable

  to the stranger

      on the skyline

NIGHT GARDEN OF YES & DREAMING

These poems
they are things that I do
in the dark
reaching for you
whoever you are
and
are you ready?

—JUNE JORDAN, These Poems

You never tell all the secrets when you're trying to get free.

—IMANI PERRY

The Ultra-Black Fish

Two hundred metres down, the light stops.
Many deep-sea creatures alive at this level
of the ocean have developed the ability to create
light for themselves. This is known as *bioluminescence.*
Others, on the contrary, contribute to the darkness
by adding themselves to it. Ultra-black fish are
one example, & in 2020 sixteen varieties of these were
~~discovered~~ captured. The level of pigment in their
skin was so high that it was found to absorb 99.956%
of the light that touched it. Karen, a marine biologist,
~~made the discovery~~ came across them by accident.
Instead of hauling up the deep-sea crabs she had been
searching for, her net produced a fang-toothed fish that
wouldn't show up in a photograph. Held, later, in a tank
under two strobe lights, the fish became a living black hole,
with no discernible features beyond the opacity of its
silhouette. As though it had cut itself out of the image & left.
Scientists believe that the fish developed their invisibility
to aid them in escaping their predators. Another theory
suggests that the obscurity of ultra-black fish enables them
to more successfully catch their prey. It is likely that both
ideas are true. Commentators ~~on their discovery~~ have also
speculated that the chemical structure of the pigment could serve
the development of military & defence technologies.
Nothing was said, however, about how ultra-black fish find
& enter into relations with each other. Nonetheless, their existence
alone is evidence that, invisible as they may be to others,
they are by no means strangers to themselves.

Of the Snail & its Loveliness

1.

Once, I saw a snail so small
so young its shell was still
    transparent.

I stopped to look—I had the time
to see a thing unseen before—
    a tiny flute

a ghost of white that swayed
    within the sleeping shell,
marking time so faithfully.

Little snail,
    you'll never know what happened
outside as you dreamed.

I watched your small heart's beating
    & called my love
to come & see.

2.

Nomad of no fixed address, praise
your paradox, your calcium elasticity.
You who wander are not lost.
Home is wherever you are right now.
Everywhere you go is where you live.

3.

Let me sing of the snail
       & its loveliness, of the beauty
I have ruined underfoot,
       wincing as though the pain
were entirely mine.
       Knowing I could walk this city
in a fatal rush
       I have learned to step aside for you.
Have crouched, even, in the rain
       to move you further along your way
in the line of your direction.
       & what is care but this: to hold
that which comes too soon to harm
       & set it on a safer path.
To say *I'm sorry*, simply—
       to do this, & not dance.
To signal the way to that place
       where the skin meets itself again
or failing that, where honey
       fills the wound's red mouth;
solders a space left empty
       of love. *Love,*
this way, we might say,
       this way,
holding, sometimes, the other
       sometimes the lonely self
until it can be said, *love*,
       we are home now.

note on exiting

for Christa

each time you leave a way-things-are that thrives upon your quiet you delegitimise it in a number of manners. you do this firstly by removing it from whatever position of integrity it occupied in your mind. this is the interior departure & so the most crucial. perhaps the way-things-are was in the realm of the acceptable, once. or simply: it needed work & you believed the effort to be possible & worthy of your prolonged & specific expense. this being so: forgive yourself. gently. but put the myth down. today you are leaving the faith.

now that you have made the first departure you are prepared for the second: your leaving with your body, your physical being, your image & likeness, in the manner that best suits. go with whatever works. behold, now, your purposeful absence from the masthead, from the recipient list, from the brochure, front & centre; rejoice! in your departure from keeping up appearances, which is not meaningful work. & it may be useful at this stage to know that you owe no grand goodbyes; that the simplicity of your leaving is resounding enough. with this action you affirm your wherewithal to exist outside of the way-things-are. this is not something that is easy to do. the way-things-are grins benevolently upon that knowledge. it trusts that it is safe insofar as you are unable to conceive of your life being otherwise. that you might paint a different landscape in your head was always possible, but deemed unlikely. even less probable was the possibility that you might not only envision but also act.

but if you have the safety & the means, you leave. & in doing so you declare to yourself & others present that as far as you are able you will not rely upon what harms you for the shaping of *your one wild and precious life*. worry not. the [   ] supremacist capitalist [*insert* -ist] [*insert* -ist] patriarchy is working faultlessly today, running at full service; no disruptions, even with your small axe in its back. but what a beautiful day for a signal failure. how wholesomely the morning seeks a paper jam, a screw loose, a car that won't start this time around; tabula rasa for your joy.

the light is coming in through the glass, the sill is warm with its touch, & some of us are learning how to quit. there will be no business as usual if that business is not of love. there will be no business as usual if that business is not of love. there will be no business as usual today. love is our only business. forever & ever, *ase*.

Dreaming is a Form of Knowledge Production

Nobody's immune to their ego taking the wheel.
Dreaming is a form of knowledge production
& they don't want it to be that easy for us.
As in: lay your head on a pillow

                      wake up holding
something new. I said what I said, not what you say
I said. Pigs are outside the house, but next door
this time. It's not something our relationship
will be able to survive. He doesn't show it, the cat,
but he loves me so. He has the gene but it hasn't
kicked in yet. Another thousand years. All thinking
& no feeling. Shut up about Freud.

dear little b,

I love to see you sat there
pregnant with promise
& nobody's business:

be bodacious if you feel like it,
be camouflaged, if not.

some might say you should be louder, bolder, tall.
uppercase & camera-ready. but little b, you're weary,

aren't you, of being counted in the wrong kinds of ways.
besides, haven't you been capital forever? haven't you

been asterisked for far too long? *no longer,
or not since, or not enough*, some might think

& let them think it, but as for me, little b
I'll be blunt now:

I like the way you lay low
the way you stay low
& keep shooting.

Air

Friend, I saw you sitting
at the window of yourself

high up in the loft
watching it all go on without you.

I was ice & you were almost shadow.
I waved like a child on a passing boat.

Unsure of whether or not this counts
I want us to remember the unreadable air.

How it waits to be recast
by the touch of our lungs—

our breath alone,
a most humble poem:

in, out, the couplet we write
without thinking. Don't go.

We must stay alive
to our place in the family

of green & breathing things
that use even our sighs

to make sweetness from light.
What grace. Allow what is simple

to be simple. Accept it as
truth. Quiet as it's kept
we help the trees to breathe too.

fabula

for the luminaries

1. *offering*

she gives herself
    to the earth.

    ants & woodlice
        electric, their movement

           astonished, ecstatic
    at the offering of her.

    she knows what they say
though they speak a different tongue.

    she lies on the split seed of dawn, (g)listening
        her skin stunned, static

           beginning to spark; darkening still.
    how she is solar. she swallows the light.

    'I do not know this language,
I am new here,' she says,

'but I lie in the sun
    & remember.'

2. *circles*

there are dark thoughts   & there are dark nights

dark in the shadows under freight trains

& there are dark nights

there is a dark that grows   itself

(winter dark)

& there are dark hours, days

there is dark humour

& there is dark light

there is dark that moves,

dark matter, boundless

& more dark, still

lovely

& deep wood-dark.

there are dark waters, landless

or there were, once,

& will be again—   *again*   *again*   *again*.

there is womb dark,

dark moon dark

        & there are dark circles, cycles.

& so it is,   & so it is: always   the outset matches the ending,

                             a dark snake with her omega in her mouth.

        & so it is,   always the dusk sings the dark of its dreamtime,

the dust of the end makes the clay of the start

      a dark,   malleable work are we,   aren't we?

there are dark hours, days   & there is dark light.

& these are dark thoughts

& these are dark cycles

& still,
we are awake.

my love, we are awake yet
& we will   again.

3. *towards a black mirror*

object responsibility
so   we've seen how, again, the black female body is the prototypical
object against which [   ] female subjectivity, therefore *womanhood*, is defined,
& how therefore insofar as black women are seen to exist in excess of that object
responsibility—whether for appearing possessed of their own sexuality, beauty or
agency, or for directly rebelling against or naming the construction into which they
have been written—in such cases, they are liable to be misread &/or punished.

ontology
western ontology as that in which there must always be opposites—*its kingdom for
some opposites!*—wherein it finds itself always on the victorious team of a series of
binaries, everything from this & *that*; winner & *loser*; human & *animal*; being & *thing*.
black female object responsibility as always to be *that, loser, animal, thing*, which
makes possible, primordially births the possibility of this, winner, human, being—
without which . . . well, now what?

seeing, knowing, seeing
seeing as this is the case;
knowing it to be the case as her back has carried it;
seeing as the binary denies her a self never mind a room of her own the birth of
that self depends upon so dearly depends upon the refusal the rejection of the
binary in order to exist in some semblance of wholeness. what might that look
like? that is, in order to enter to emerge as I she must dance she must two-step that
move called *both &*—you know how it goes. *both &* as body & mind. nature &
nurture. here & there. self & other. male & female. now & then. matter & spirit. they &
them. as he & her. she & her. me & mine & you & you all. as we & them & we & 'nem &
them & us. as you & you all & you lot & you man & I & I. & I & I. *& who am I anyway?*

[75]

a question, since

unreflected as such, what might it mean to have a blackened mirror, a black mirror? since, as we know, black absorbs all light & denies its outward reflection, it is the polishedness of this black surface that gives this black mirror its mirrorness. into this inner black mirror she looks & she who looks back out is not fully seen & yet she who looks back out appears fully; deep it. she appears not entirely there but in her closebutnotquiteness she is there in entirety. & all that is seen of her is not all there is, the perfect lighting, the complete image, is not most honest for her true likeness abhors a vacuum, a [   ] room under harsh light; what can she say in such incarcerations, such interrogations but nothing, as is her right; her true likeness lives wherein she knows her self as much by what she sees of her self as what she cannot see, which with this blackened mirror might just about mean anything, thus everything, held as she is in her half-reflection, with room enough left for the possible. with scope enough for the imaginary. dark & potent as space itself. she looks, she sees & pleased, then, she says: *there now, see, here I am.*

4. *the night garden*

there is nothing left, one says, *the water is ruined & the land is taken*

we are what's left, says another

nightly like this, it happens

assembling from Nowhere, the women work
beside one another, unnumbered, their faces less obvious
than their outlines, tucked under the smile of a crescent moon

their humming sculpts the air like a night bloom
it steadies & keeps them warm

we do not know if this is our end or our birth, a voice says

it is too soon to tell, replies another
but we know, at least, our work, they sing in chorus
it is what will have had to happen

death workers they are, busy
performing, mycelial, the art of breakage & burial
& decomposition; the reduction of structure to mineral & salt

down in the warm dark of the soil is the future
they must make new soil if they wish to live
they must sow what they themselves may not eat

the work is long & seemingly without end
they arc their hours with small laughter; they stop to sing & rest & story

where I come from,
there are weeks of the year
during which our drumming stops
it is decreed by the seers
that during this time
there must be peace
if we do not heed this,
our seeds will not grow

the hours pass; the years & minutes

it has been done

yes, it has been done before

I know of a people who made a home of water
to escape being stolen across the sea
they took to the water

took their lives & didn't die

they made a village on a lake, their people say
it is a place where babies swim
before walking, where
when strangers come with cameras
they turn their heads—

still refuse capture

yes

beloved, & what is the name of this place

[78]

it is called ████████
& it means 'we are safe'

they listen, listen again

                             it is so quiet here; here where we hear so much

only to what the darkness asks of us will we answer
we who are wayward & not astray
we who are wary of searchlights under which
seeing ourselves is no kin to being with one another
we who are watchful of eyebeams vivid
vivid they may be, but hollow

                             yet touch is trust, is all
touch is risk, is hope, is love

                       is love in hope of love so circular
                           we must be circular
                        a whole & cornerless love

breathe, breathe

                             all begins here.

if sound begets word—
if word is beginning—
                if breath sufficient—
if word begets world then worldsmiths are they,
                        in search of otherwise—

fugitive, below
the dreadful scope of the visible, beneath
the wingèd singing of bats, at the lower end of sound—
they live like this,
subjunctively: *to live*—
they live in this, a grammar alive
in furtherance of life
in service of its likelihood
they braid the future like a child's hair
singing &
sewing bright dark seeds into it.

f   ork a path   glitch   a lineage split a line   dis   cord to cause a break
to make a new chain   a novel habit   for the nervous system   ritual to re
call   entrain a new genetic   & calibrate DNA otherhow re-member   make
memory available for future recovery   make myth for later ceremony   whisper
sing   by heart   till morning we are   darklight & livingness unfathom
able   we are   nothing we have seen before   we are light for we drink
     it   in   we are light   for we let it go   bless the day
& the night   & the mystery in we   & in you   & in you   & in you

Acknowledgements

Thank you to the editors of *Ambit, bath magg, Granta, Magma, The Guardian, The Nation, ZYZZYVA, MAP Magazine,* the *Poets in Bed* podcast, *The Rialto, London Review of Books, Tongue, Ten: Poets of the New Generation* and *Stand* for giving homes to several poems that now appear in this book.

To Apples and Snakes, Arts Council England, Free Word, People's Palace Projects, Instituto Sacatar, the Hedgebrook Foundation, the British Council, the V&A Museum, Palestine Festival of Literature and the Technē Doctoral Training Partnership I am grateful for gifts of space, study, exchange and travel across the years. I have been shaped by these permanently—from London to Bahia; from Whidbey Island to Hebron.

To the following, for many encouragements: Dan Simpson; Jacob Sam-La Rose and the Barbican Young Poets family; Bernardine Evaristo, Nathalie Teitler and the Complete Works family; Octavia Poetry Collective; Nii Ayikwei Parkes; the late Professor Atukwei Okai; Kwame Dawes; M. NourbeSe Philip; Catherine Smith; Joy Francis; Joanna Brown; Sarah Perry; Kayo Chingonyi; Dave Coates; Jack Underwood; Mary Jean Chan; Sarala Estruch; R. A. Villanueva; Nick Makoha; Natalie Diaz; Terri Ochiagha; and Lavinia Greenlaw.

At Aitken Alexander Associates: thank you, Emma Paterson, my deepest appreciation for your kind, fine eye, and your belief in my writing. Thank you, Monica MacSwan, for always being on hand to help. There is so much more to come.

Immeasurable gratitude to my publishers, thank you: to Lavinia Singer, for reaching out in the first place; to Matthew Hollis, for your deeply intuitive understanding of this work, for an editorial journey that left me sharper; to Rali Chorbadzhiyska, throughout, and the Faber & Faber family at large. Thank you, John Freeman, and the wider Knopf family, for the love you've shown this book all along; I am so humbled.

To Kevin Quashie, without whose tenderness, scope and practice this work might not have found its form; for your kindness and grace. This book is also for you. Thank you, likewise, to DJ Lynnée Denise for bringing *The Sovereignty of Quiet* into my orbit at exactly the right moment, and for a brilliance that is entirely your own.

To my better mirrors: Marcelle Mateki Akita, Sabrien Amrov, Stephanie Fada-hunsi, Janna Chowdhury, Belinda Zhawi, Sumia Juxun, Bayan Goudarzpour, Remi Graves, Myah Jeffers, Hannah Turner Wallis, Sarah Lasoye, Ama Rouge and Theresa Lola. Thank you, also, Jay Gao, Raymond Antrobus, Will Harris, Keith Jarrett, Gboyega Odubanjo, Omar Bynon, Caleb Azumah Nelson, Jamal Mehmood and many more. A deep bow.

To Christa Welsh, for saying *when you love something, you want it to live*; for loving me.

To my family, embodied and ancestral, near and far; to Mum, Dad, Richard, Abigail and Elliot. Thank you for raising a writer in me.

To Timothy, for you; for the beauty of the life we have made by hand, quietly, together. Love is too small a word.

Notes on the Poems

'How Not to Disappear'

This poem's epigraph borrows words spoken by Evidence Joel in an interview with Sky News following the disappearance of her son, Richard Okorogheye, from their London home. Okorogheye, aged 19, was reported missing in March 2021. His body was subsequently recovered from a pond in Epping Forest in the weeks following.

'[   ] noise'

For its ability to cut through environmental sound, white noise is used in the sirens of police cars, ambulances and fire engines, and is also known to have been used as a tool during interrogations and torture. In its power to disrupt atmospherically or occlude in totality, white noise might perhaps be thought of as a sonic of distress, a marker of the state and its attendant emergencies.

'black noise'

Black noise is a phrase used to describe an absence of noise. It refers to quiet or near and total silence inflected with random instances of noise.

'Pandemic vs Black Folk'

The italicised lines in the final verse directly echo those from Lucille Clifton's poem 'cruelty. don't talk to me about cruelty', which read *now i watch myself whenever i enter a room. / i never know what i might do.*

'note on exiting'

The line *'your one wild and precious life'* is taken from the poem 'The Summer Day' by Mary Oliver, while the late bell hooks is referenced for her phrase 'imperialist white-supremacist capitalist patriarchy'.

'fabula'

Elements of this sequence nod towards several writers and artists whose practice is rooted in a black feminist poetics of being. Among them are: Lorraine O'Grady (particularly her essay 'Olympia's Maid: Reclaiming Black Female Subjectivity'); Tina Campt, her 'Grammar of Black Futurity', and 'anteriority'—from which the words *what will have had to happen* are sampled; Saidiya Hartman and her meditations on the fugitive and wayward; Christina Sharpe's 'wake work' and wakefulness; along with Simone Browne, Legacy Russell, Alexis Pauline Gumbs, and many more to whom I am in gratitude.

Also present in this poem are two happenings of quiet worlding that, though potentially appearing fabled, are real. The first is the Ga indigenous customary period of *adu nmaa* ('we have planted the seeds'), during which time there is a ban on drumming and noisemaking in Accra, Ghana. I thank my mother for holding this knowledge and language; for continuing to share it with me.

The second is a reference to a maroon community in West Africa. In the spirit of that place, and of this book, I feel it less important to name that place than to affirm, simply, that it exists.

Further Reading

The Sovereignty of Quiet: Beyond Resistance in Black Culture
Kevin Quashie

Sula
Toni Morrison

In the Wake: On Blackness and Being
Christina Sharpe

Wayward Lives, Beautiful Experiments
Saidiya Hartman

Black Utopias: Speculative Life and the Music of Other Worlds
Jayna Brown

Listening to Images
Tina Campt

Selected Poems
Una Marson

In Praise of Shadows
Jun'ichirō Tanizaki

Noopiming: The Cure for White Ladies
Leanne Betasamosake Simpson

Selected Works
María Sabina

Victoria Adukwei Bulley is a poet, a writer and an artist. An alumna of the Barbican Young Poets and recipient of an Eric Gregory Award, Bulley has held residencies in the United States and Brazil, and in London at the Victoria and Albert Museum. Her debut chapbook, *Girl B*, was published by the African Poetry Book Fund in 2017. She is currently a Techne doctoral scholar at Royal Holloway, University of London.

A NOTE ON THE TYPE

This book was set in Minion, a typeface produced by the Adobe Corporation specifically for the Macintosh personal computer and released in 1990. Designed by Robert Slimbach, Minion combines the classic characteristics of old-style faces with the full complement of weights required for modern typesetting.

Printed and bound by
Berryville Graphics
Berryville, Virginia